Saw Horse

SAW HORSE

MICK VRANICH

POEMS 1990–1999

Doorjamb Press

Doorjamb Press
P. O. Box 1296
Royal Oak, MI 48068-1296

Cover design by Sherry Hendrick & Jim Johnson
Typesetting design by Christine Monhollen
Back photo by Sherry Hendrick
© Calligraphy by Yoko Nomura

First Edition
Printed in USA by
Cushing-Malloy
1350 N. Main Street
Ann Arbor, Michigan 48107

Distributed by
Small Press Distribution
1341 Seventh Street
Berkeley, CA 94710-1403

ISBN: 1-884118-05-4

Library of Congress Cataloging-in-Publication Data
Saw Horse/ Poems 1990-1999/Mick Vranich—1st ed.

CONTENTS

MUD

STICKS

Hammer

NAILS

for Leonard Peltier

MUD

SUN DOWN SUN UP

another notch off the slice
of time here on the edge of
the millennium looks like we
got more to do than we set
out to do when we first put
the spirit boat into the water
yanked on the lines the sails
filled with the sweet winds
of dawn but the storm kicked up
so unpredictably darkness crashed
down like a muddy heel
we had to find the other source
of strength to propel the vision
fling it through space like
an alchemical flashlight
winging it over the lakes.

Not A Scratch

what did you put on the shelf last
a cup and a spoon to stir you
out of sleep into the morning
it was the last flight of stairs
where the sweat got between your
fingers and the trunk on your back
the up rooted tree trunk on her back
you saw it today didn't you
before the water boiled
the horizon rises out of the
darkness. i parked the station
wagon in the gravel parking lot
behind the building it didn't
all fall apart no whole to begin with
depleted from scavenging to find
moorings some place to loop the rope
rings around tie downs to keep my feet
on the ground a radical flat tire pulls
me across the path of the on coming tidal
wave of dreams there without words
carving initials in the glass
the window shatters right before
my eyes. so there it was the face
keeps reappearing in the middle
of sleep trudging through deep snow
the howling close behind the footsteps
covered before they are seen
just trying to make a song
move at the same speed as before
but nothing was written down
no notations not even a scratch

or two to give the impression
of how the song should go
it's all chopped up and inconsistent
the wind is so intense i can't see
anything white out feeling my way
with each step frozen in place
beyond the sensations of your own skin
rely on the other who only arrives
when pretending ends no trace
of a past no memory
only the glow of the driving snow
aiming at the destination.

LITTLE TOO LATE

you could try to say something
about the observance but it would
only confuse the flow of data
to the bank accumulation suffocates
the sleeping victims without
a single wound on the body
of knowledge fill in scratch out
a living the characters' roles are
all short lived most get no coverage
at all a trail of numbers leading
to the drop off point
but you got there a little too late
to contain the explosion that must
have occurred to cause the damage
you can't see the apparent
keep going back to the scene
right before falling asleep
the seat tilted back as far
as it will go the windows fogged
from the freeze in the night
some rest stop with a couple trucks
idling clicking exhaust pipe gate
popping up and down as the trucks
idle puffs of exhaust clouds of smoke.

LIVE FROM THEN

he went some where once
unaware of an arrival
maintaining a direction
no arrival issued for the
trip over the Golden Gate
right at dawn the sun
coming up over Alcatraz
vast blue water
to the west.

ONE FALSE MOVE

fill in the blank back in the space
empty the room so the walls are bare
just the door and a couple of windows
the door is open to the night
vibrating from the celestial arrangements
of light and dark
the path is crooked through the trees
barely visible at first until your eyes
adjust the ground is dry and makes
noises underfoot no sense
of direction except moving forward
for now out of reach
a receptor to the currents of wind
gusting in twists of air around your head
not much to say when it's this quiet
no report of events some where else
stop here and build a fire
wait for a messenger
to show up with the note
the next place to go
the words get smaller and smaller
start to look the same
the nature of the beast of language
without a face transparent and constant
the method of capture involves
the silence around each word
cracking open to reveal the sound
a nest of words crack open
like fresh blue eggs
the instinct to eat the first offering
dropped into the open mouth

wakefulness to the universe
the departure from behind
the fragile walls into the burst
of air and light even on this dark path
the light is steaming off the stars
reflecting in the still water.

now is already gone
i can't recount a single incident
bouncing off the walls that suddenly appear
a scar here or there from the collision
one false move the bag of bones
against the gravel and dirt
watching the birds pick around
for seeds in dried leaves
wake from the crackle
of the pheasant's voice
stumble around to maintain
this upright position ridiculous as it is
to be standing here
with this flat vision.

MEMORY LAPSE

the wind is picking up
sheets of plywood
from the roof like
the old house of cards
playing solitaire on the cardboard
table top down in the basement
the view of garbage cans
between the buildings
the alley to the mountain top
one card on the other
all the faces turned away
from the light
only think for a second
then get back
in the tire tracks.

SPIDER WEB

the thaw can't be here yet
just into january the squalls
danced right around the great
lakes water pushing at the gates
of the storm front throwing
the white blanket over the sky
scrapers less than ants it doesn't
work to say as small as them
their balance so much more precise
than our rude approach to every
thing else alive around us
something is on fire or it's not
two states of being here at
the edge of bursting into flames
a few more breaths from the bellows
of the nuclear blast too obvious
when there can be so many other
reasons for the plutonium dice
hanging from the rear view mirror
the relentless automobile in the
post punk ghost dance.
look over there in the bushes
right by the pool of grease and blood
making the organic muck on your boots
it's too quiet for there to be anyone
else around here did you see it there
more dismembered pieces of the mechanical
anatomy the surface of your skin still
twitching from the presence of some other
you can't explain with your language
disconnected from the voice
that keeps a vibration in the air

of the darkness before the sun
is suppose to rise.
the fire is down to glowing coals
getting the last heat before crawling
under a rock where the spider is
leaving for the place she weaves her
web through the night.

TUNNEL VISION

in the vague light
of the glove compartment bulb
the map lines indistinguishable
mingling with each other
the words a blur
over the highways and rivers
looking for the symbol
of a tent at midnight
rolling down the mountain.
resting your head somehow
on the armrest in the backseat
the door seems closed tight
the rest of your body
would hold you in if
the door flung open
going around the stiff curve
the road just a little slick
from the start of the ice storm.
there's always the possibility
she just won't start
for some unknown reason
everything was fine when
i shut her off to go in
buy a pack of cigarettes
coffee in a plastic cup
tastes even worse when it's cold
like this waiting for something
to change. the thing came out
of no where dead center
in your lights all you do

is maintain because there is
no thought involved not meant
for interpretation or the sense
of control it will be out
of control until the other side
arrives or it doesn't.

WINDOW REPAIR

captured by your own body
forced to pay attention
to the fragile parts
sitting at this altar
called a window
watching the blue jay
pick up a peanut
off the sawhorse
on the back porch
up hill down hill
the level killing field
staring at a piece of blue
through the hole in the wall
morning must be here
the sun must be shining
burning up in the fury
the way it does so
constantly we think
is a steady stream of heat
and power getting closer
we got to go and fix some
broken windows in the apartment
house on second avenue
single room occupant
old folks home battleship
gray hallways army green trim
we can only look at the sky
we can't be in it
we are in it at ground level
the wind is gentle today
everything stays in place
for awhile.

THE DAY BEFORE JOHN LENNON WAS SHOT
for Bill Hodgson

the photographs are so scratched up
you can't tell who's sitting there
from the rock face of the mountain
staring out baked in the blue light
of the full moon the one before this
one when all the muscles in you erupted
flexed and made the rest of your body
squirm and shiver the bones in your feet
turned black like long dead branches
tangled under your skin replacing words
dropping under your tongue falling from
some spot unseen destination hurling toward
you but how could you know you were headed
there. where are you playing tonight Bill
we hit on a joint at the kitchen table
by the window looking down on the back yard
the old brick garage the alley everything covered with
the new snow a man picking
through the dumpster down by the market
i can barely see through the falling
snow the last light of day still illuminating
from the crystals Bill fills his glass
from a quart of Pabst and i top off mine
with Gallo burgundy light up a cigarette
after freeing a plume of herb smoke from my
lungs Bill always has one of his acoustic
guitars in the kitchen on its own chair
he picks up the big blond bodied Gibson plays for
awhile a piece he's working up for sunday night.
i thing i'm slipping it feels

that way the knotted rope hanging
down the rock face like a tear
hand prints on the cave wall
the phone rings i reach over
pick it up Bill's still playing
singing tramp on the street hello
yeah i'll be there later what time
you going the rope with the knots
twists in the wind it can't be
anymore clear the way it moves
from here even outer space wears out
the arms of the rotating space station
dramatically lit lamp shades the cigarette
smoke drifting through the yellow light
who cares what you eat crawling out
the hatch with connecting cord rolling
out into the cosmic night cluttering
the stillness with your reconnaissance
the wrong wrench in your pocket to fix
the crack in the body of the craft
the nuts just fly off you don't know
which way to turn who threaded this
backwards your cord is kinked.

LET MY HEAD DROP

tired awake for a long time
get up stand on the memory
of what it is to be here
walk out and be real
i soaked my face in a sea
of wine and drowned and died
away now i walk around
in this body that went
through the waves piled up
on the rocks the messages
ending having to speak
for some unknown force
where all the voices collect
in the places where they
run to get the remaining water

more than likely no one gets out
the incarceration revealed in every glance
the vacant morning darkness lingers around
the edges of the trees no color a density
of darkness migrating through the branches
bare for at least a month the birds aren't
awake yet waiting for the first song
moment of blending into the progress
of the light that is not here yet
crawl out from under the skin
of your own eyes
back again there are many ways
to sing the thing through you
get to the next circle on the
radio band some other language

some other rendition a misconception
to think you understand the starts
and stops the other place the sounds
originate where the water runs
in the opposite direction for one
thing the needles vibrate to what
you call the altered setting
the pigeon snatched up by the hawk
in the side yard a couple pushes
and she's up in the oak
tearing off a piece of back.

PERFECT REPLICA

the cruel and monotonous accumulation
of details backing up in my brain unreconciled
facts thrown out over the air waves or where
ever they go now through cables under the
ground bounced off satellites accelerated
beyond the speed of light some such shit
just today i found out they're going to use
cow eggs as the perfect medium for cloning
endangered species so don't worry about those
creatures anymore they can make you a condor
out of a cow's egg and the same day Carl Perkins
passed over to the real world hope they didn't
freeze his DNA for look alikes.

SONIC GEOGRAPHY

el paso salsa yellow freightliner
at the edge of Ohio Ray Brown and
Duke Ellington on the box in the
truck back and forth talking to each
other little rattles from different
spots in the steel body heading for
New York to do a couple shows pitch
the tent let the animals out beat
the drum beat the bushes get the word
out Black River floats by just before
falling out for the rest of side one
you're going to need a monster tow
truck to get out of there in that
little room again snow knee deep
drifting to shoulder height everything
in sight is rotating around the invisible
center proof of the vortex make it
easy on yourself the proof is on
the flood plain talk to the lowlands.

ORIGINAL CAST

the migration of snakes
no one knowing why it is
they decide to travel in one
direction all at once
maybe a thousand snakes
the sound of skin and ribs
against the earth
standing like a stick among them
their flesh pushes against my ankles
over my feet like thick water
the rippling skin and ribs
start to move waves of dirt
and sand and stones made into
trailing paths behind them
as they move together
moving slowly over the earth
they tell each other
how it is closing in on all sides
like it is for us
standing here in the sea of snakes
there is a calm
wake from your dream
move the walls away
stare in the hole
at your feet
the captive heart
pulled down from the sky.

FORGET IT

only a few items left to mark the spot
where i'd sit look out on the street
covered with snow tonight the cars are
stopped everywhere you can't hear any
motors running the lights are out from
the lines icing up but still too warm
on the edge of the arctic the polar bears
coming into town to see what's happening
get a bite to eat don't know what
direction to head their fur is rough
stained with dirt it's a shame
how they looked that's not your concern
i shouldn't have brought it up
the wrong focus these days
forgetfulness is the remedy for pain
look the other way if you don't like
what you see who needs a bear
on the street wandering around with her cubs
sticking her nose in the air
sniffing out the wind for a sign
where to turn in the traffic
who needs her around to confuse your lists
get the stun gun get the net and pointed
stick rearrange the silverware
she'll be gone soon
her and all her unruly kind don't fit
the program being loose like that
prowling around on the black ice
you forgot who to call for help.

RIMBAUD'S LEG
for Jim Gustafson

he was getting ready to leave
San Francisco after seven years
trying to make a go of it but
things seem to be collapsing around
him and inside him lifting boxes
of car parts out of the semi trailer
loading the parts into the pick up
delivering the stuff around SF to make
a buck then wandering the streets of
north beach at night meeting up with
Jim at Vesuvios going out in the alley
to smoke a joint going back inside
sitting at the window booth watching
the action on Columbus Avenue working
up some strategy for the band a gig
at Mabuhay Gardens a gig at the Stud
where the queens and lumberjacks hit
poppers on the dance floor the band
combusting on the stand pushing the
sonic mass over the edge unraveling
ropes of notes to match the song he
was singing about dwelling on the burning
planet after the show two queens got on
top of the van and wouldn't get down
after all the gear was packed their lip
stick smeared panty hose torn laughing
hysterically everybody laughing a 3 am
Jim along for the ride stirring things
up to see if he could get the queens off
the top of the van to dance with him

they do the dancing bear routine with Jim
until they get worn out everybody climbs
in drive off to stash the gear head over
to the mission for tacos and beer.

CUT OUT

the dream of the orange duck
walking on the blue sky
as close to me as this ceiling
looking at me with his head cocked
to one side like he was studying
my stillness below him
these characters don't show up
that often for me
there was a scarlet bird
that flew in close circles
around my head when i
had a three day fever
on Potrero Hill in a room
i was renting from Cliff
red as the cardinal in the snow
red as the blood i could see
behind my eyes in the night
that didn't want to end
laying in the sweating bed.

NOT MUCH TO GO ON

bombardment with the data
keep the doors locked tight
so the gun can't get inside
your face tonight is blank
the secrets are over here
one thing hard to believe
when the door opens
the figure is not human
fur coat spotted with snow
the eyes of the wolf
say how long is left
the figure's wings are folded
under the yellow feathered robe
only part of the dream returns.

WAR ROOMS

figure out a way to get down
how the street smelled how
the sound ringing in my ears
drove my metabolism how
the mushrooms in Big Sur make
it feel like your heart is going
to leave your body pounding against
your ribs in the little cabin
in the redwood trees the darkness
the pounding heart the cells
of the mushrooms releasing into
your cells throwing out everything
occupies your body makes you start
over wade through the pounding
following the sounds squeezing out
the last drop of assumptions
of where you are in the arms
of the redwoods in the roots
of the redwoods the convulsions
making your body disappear
the last drop of energy turned
to soil settling down able to
see the walls of the room get up
walk out sit down at the base
of the tree and fall asleep
figure out a way to tell what
the tree passed through me
what i left in the trunk
a hand full of faces in photographs
fighting against the war
with wood guitars paint brushes

secret meetings in the basement
raised with the atom bomb
under the bed dancing around
sweat in the love music
breathing life into us
you've seen the pictures
they show the tribal dancing
they show the bombs exploding
casting shadows in the mushroom
cloud the monks on fire figure
out who was walking around
in this body in the streets
in the war daze.

ANYWHERE IS THE CENTER
"...but anywhere is the center of the world."
— Black Elk

if i did everything the way
i decided to do it right
at that instant without
all the sorting and straining
over the consequential implications
where it will lay how the chips
fall when you hit the floor
the glass filling the bar room
must have been a shot gun
blast or a cinder block
thrown off the back
of the passing pick up truck
with the tailgate down
some crazy looking camouflage
you are wearing out
your low gear creeping
out of the mud ruts
if i walk back and forth
in the room for a long
time for only a couple
of days without stopping
not moving fast just back
and forth in the room
watching the light start
to show up on the floor
after it was so dark
it is like there is no floor.

BROKEN HOOP

get the momentum to make it up
the mountain not enough time
to find the way through
the falling rocks and rain
pounding forced out of the hoop
left floating around with the
radio blasting out the same old
bed of broken sticks log jam
the earth can wait us out
the turbulence mysterious as sand
shifting mountains around rearranging
the map like a finger painting you
make on the floor on newsprint.
the marching hordes the conquering
forces shooting into the sky propelled
beyond capture in the flashing screen
the momentary dissolve sliding into
the sea eating away at the roots
stealing the air you open your mouth
there's nothing left to replenish
a single cell fame is routine
the signposts taking you where
you've been all along
a heart dried up in your chest
resents being part of you.
explain what the picture shows
the mouths opening and closing like
doors swinging in the wind the cold
blowing through the room rain
pounding on the glass trying to
strike a match to see where we're
at shadows dancing around in the

brief light go back down the crooked
path when the light is gone sitting
in the dark forgetting what i said
to start with the picture thrown away
didn't make any sense to talk about
it in the first place pressing the point
beyond return looking for an out
casting doubt about the outcome
incomplete not a spot not the finish
unraveling plots with no one saying
a word to each other wandering off
like the shadows in the match light
was what i was trying to tell you
about how we looked in the snapshot.

STICKS

PASSAGE

the only voices that will talk
whisper about what they see outside
in the stand of trees along the edge
of the thin river pacing in the night.

BLESSING IN DISGUISE

the crowded sanctuary of angels
and demons illuminate the brilliance
of the strings
'inspirations and visions condemned'
William Blake says
that is where he lives
in these places some knot of roots
made into the form of the two legged.
the voice that shows up
is on a long journey
so it only speaks
for a minute
then heads out on this
trip it's on to who knows
where i heard it this time
caught a couple of words.
from that point retrieving
each part of the sound
that makes the words
pulling your hands
through the world
seeing bones break
and heal before your eyes
while you wait to find
balance feeling the ridges
of your spine
the map of mountains
cut by white water
dried sumac leaves
a red blanket on the clothes line
'hold infinity in the palm of your
hand' William Blake said

stuff blowing around under the overpass
the words stay buried in the dirt
under your feet changing footing
through the seasons of wind
carving the creases in the corners
of your eyes watching the man
pick through the dumpster
after the thanksgiving parade
down Woodward Avenue
the record is temporary
fingers sorting the trash
for something the body can
live on boxes of chicken bones
reading them like sticks
in the path.

FIND THE CLOCK

i thought i heard something
tonight but it wasn't outside
and it wasn't inside
back to the spot in the circle
where did it all fall to
like snow that was just here
now the ground is sprouting
green the cardinal starts talking
about the sun going down.

ACTION FILM

isolated from the big flow
capsized in icy water
there is a distant light
flashing point of land
out of reach holding
on to the keel in the dark
is how the movie starts
you have to do this stuff
for yourself with the flood
of battles projected through
the blue glow the constant
you use to determine
your position where you
fit in the groove or you
don't fit at all the internal
dialogue the constant
that pulls at the flesh
of your face slowly makes
the creases contour
to the face
of your skull.
just trying to tell you
what it is like in here
with the swinging things
that are suppose to be
stable makes the whole
picture confused.
the lack of any way
to keep track of the change
at the moment not there
but on the high ridge

overlooking us you've seen
the view on the television
show about nature the wonder
of the expedition over the
mountain with clanking steel
swords and leather over the
horses back bone pulling away
from the place where they know
they are going to carry the
lead bullet into the heart
the death flame a breath of
fire and blue smoke
the smell of rancid stew.

As Above So Below

for Richard Montoya

stand by for further
instructions when your
back bone becomes the pole
flex around the circle
from the sky from the ground
this is too much nothing more
the lights turn up keep remaking
the lines shave the edges
so the thorns lay down
flat before you rub your
hand over the brink
your whole body goes over
the side into the water
is cold the rain is not
clear but slow and thick
like thinking all the time
the smoky window from a dark
winter the nights getting
shorter like tonight's rain
the moon is smoking her pipe
the trail of smoke
is the night cloud
that drifts past in
the light of her face.

CIGAR BOX

warm like it must be for
the feathers inside this cigar box
fall from above drifting from up
there to land in this cigar box.

BLOOD IS BLUE

as definitive as a barbed hook
dangling under water
the yellow of the robin's beak
close to the roadside
screening out the clumps
of clay from the sand
the hawk lands in my head
today but won't say
anything stopped where
her wings hold the air
her tail feathers
spread in a fan.
yeah it is uneven
the recesses of darkness
pulling at the door
with all your strength
it won't open
the flames roar around
on the other side
the wall of water
crashing at the window
what you want to say
only every other door
will open for you
the ones in between
release your own pulse
as it looks around
like a snake in the sand
headed for the shade
of rocks and stray shoots
of grass before the sun

heats the crystals where
the flesh burns from
inside from below the
surface the same pulse
that puts you to sleep
dreams on its own
you are there somewhere
with it you are it.

FIRST CLASS
for Paul Schwarz

staring beyond the grip
of the glass between
your eyes and the stars
how we all reach the
light in our own time
running into a constant
horizon catching our
breath as we go closer
to the edge of what
is our time lapsed
in this world like
the slow pictures of
the petals opening
closing opening closing
then falling off.
remember making pictures
of the stars and moons
on the canvas notebook
sitting in the tiny chair
with all the strangers
sitting like you at the
desks struggling
with the pencil
to make words
to make the language
and forgetting
before the anger cripples
your tongue before the
anger cripples your
soul you didn't have

that scar on your heart
yet the day dream
at the little table
in the room
full of strangers
like you.

WAITING FOR THE WINGS

waiting for the wings to spread
it just didn't happen
so the silence sow the seed
some harmony beyond our reach
among the clutter the simple
root of the weed the world
floats out to the sea of stars
the one we are on floating
like a word out in space
the chanting makes a rope out of
words dreams of tiny eyes staring
out of feathered heads.
staring at the moon
six pheasants sleeping
in the tree branches
a truck rolls down
the street shifting gears
each pheasant settles
in a chosen place
wing sounds against the branches
as they settle in for the night.

ANT IN THE TORNADO

lots of talk about
how to get some kind of program
for the skid marks on your
face organ abrasions there
must be a vicious voice
mutation of the surfaces
talking to the ants
who end up on the kitchen
sink having to carry them
out on a piece of paper
coaxing them to get on
before the storm hits
it's rumbling thunder
but no rain yet there's
one ant left still wandering
around very alert the signal
blast air raid siren funnel
cloud sighted just west of
here clearing off the spots
for implantation of more
lightning to grow out
of the ground how lightning
grows out of the ground.

HOLD OUT
for Mark Turcotte

the fiow is stopped
between the points
in the construction of bricks
of flesh in the valley
where the raven keeps
circling the smoldering fires
the ground gives off the smell
of something other than earth
everything is switched off
i've given up taking in
the pictures the voices
coming out of the boxes
maybe one line will show up
some day and i can throw
it into the river
wander back to the fire
burn the paper the line
is on so no one can find
it that's the literature
stumbling in the world
of boots kicking in faces
feed on the raven circle
above the valley
where the fires smolder
after the boys with guns
and knives came through
thrashed the people down
again another batch disposed
of the evolution has us
here in this pile
preparing for another assault.

JUST A FACE

post alcoholic visions are different
than the ones in the burning station wagon
somewhere between Nogales and Tucson Arizona
in the middle of the purple night the yellow
flames rage out of the hood walk away from it
it was just my face that was burning
it wasn't in the engine at all.

SHOES

a pair of abandoned shoes
on the shoulder in the gravel
like someone just walked out
of them like the highway
is the bed and the shoes
are at the edge of grass
is green now leaves on the trees
the turkey vulture looks down
tilts on the wind soars off
maybe she was looking at the
puffed up raccoon road kill
next to the shoes.

WHO RESCUES WHO

if you don't turn on the TV
in the drywall and formica
motel room the walls won't
just melt away the room
won't know what to do
how to act with the TV off
the smell goes away
the objects start to become
three dimensional if the TV
is off long enough the waves
are heavier than air so they
sink into the ground after
awhile if the TV is off
in the motel room the neon
sign with steel legs
walks away you follow
the tracks of concrete feet
until they vaporize in the
fluorescent blast that fires
up the night. the bird caught
in the garage looked at me
before she took off
out of my hands
i cupped her wings carefully
while they were beating
against the glass
carried her out the door
she gave me a strange glance
before she took off never
lost a feather in the whole
episode her eyes are in my
face the TV is off.

HELP ON THE WAY

passing the Horse Cave exit
just north of Nashville
are there horses in the cave
under us hooving at the stone
uncovering the precious grass
a quiet herd of buffalo
on the side of the highway
the old hawk hovering over
the ridge of cedar trees
ragged wing feathers
break the light leave
a shadow in the green branches.

THE SOLUTION

Buddha is at the back door
asking for a peanut and some corn
i give him what he wants
he takes it and goes and sits
on a log and eats then comes back
walks in and says sit down
you can't see the forest
for the trees he says you think
too much and do too little he
adjusts his fur hat looks at the
floor you wander around in a fog
most of the time confusion
is your companion so watch
who you hang out with he taps
his foot in some weird beat
starts singing like a crow
looks at me you don't know
the words to this song yet
it doesn't take practice
throw everything away you have
you think has value
throw it all away empty
the shelves empty the drawers
empty the rooms cover the floor
with cedar and sawdust and dirt
walk around in bare feet
in the snow if you have to
to feel something stop thinking
about it there is no it
give me another peanut and
a cup of cold coffee and
a cigarette i light the match

he draws slowly
blows smoke in my face makes
my hair smell sweet smoke
clouds fill the room but i can
still see his purple scarf hear
that song your wounds don't weaken
you just change how you walk
change how you open and close
your mouth to make those
words you're always talking
about the smoke clears as he
butts out the cigarette
under his foot I got to go
but I'll be back
get out of your head
before it's too late
and you're buried in all the stuff
look at that sparrow
coming down off the tree
just got back flying around
with the hawk
she picks crumbs from
between the cracks
in the bricks.

LOST IN BATTLE

so you found the small brown stone
bound in sinew like someone did it
not that long ago right there
by the stand of old cedar and pine
you could be mistaking it for a
piece of gravel from the road
a mile or so away caught in
the boot tread dropped by the trees
a small thing wedged between
the soul and the stone.

NOT THAT FAR
for George Tear

i don't reach for nothing
the desire burned out
from a sad old root
the first death
with the american flag
over his body brought
home to be buried he's
just a few blocks from
his house still what's left
of his bones are there.

DRESSED TO KILL

out the door the hoards
in sports outfits everybody
on some kind of team names
and numbers star slam dunkers
homerun hitters touch down
on the ground in shoes with
flashing lights for walking
down the dark street
on little plastic telephones
look around to see if some
body is seeing them make
the call i go home start
throwing everything away
old books weird shirts worn
out boots nuts and bolts
rubber wheels where ever
we go up in the air the smoke
is collecting just out of sight
let the fences rot rust fall over
manifest eternity with the correct
software. the world bank opens
his mouth bares his teeth
takes a bite out of the jungle
swallows her whole stomps off
kicks over the hour glass
the sand spills in the water
gets picked up by the wind
carried off in all directions
the hour hand the minute hand
second hand clothes a whole
wardrobe ten bucks with antlers.

SNAKE IN THE VIOLIN

point the remote another direction
seduction with no possible outcome
concluding where the gears seize
there is not prior knowledge about
what will arrive what form it will
take when it touches the air
for the first time. the old
chinese man sitting on a small
wooden stool in the crescent shelter
the glass store front makes in
china town in San Francisco
at midnight you can hear the song
of his two string violin with the
horse hairs rubbing in between
the strings making them harmonize
in some wave length that captures
you and pulls you to where he is
sitting making the song. after
standing at the edge of his song
in that time in the song
ends he looks right at me
here you play impossible
a cylinder the size of a soup can
cut out of mahogany
with a piece of snake skin
stretched across the top a thin
stick for a neck and a couple
tuning pegs stuck in the top
make the sound with the bow
between the strings the wooden
cylinder rests on your knee

you touch the strings to make
the notes with your left hand
move the bow with your right
impossible to make any sound
an occasional squeak or whine
no longer notes out in the air
like ribbons like he was doing
he laughs as i keep trying
when i hit a note that lasts
a second he says concentrate
on the sound concentrate.

BIRDS TALK

the birds talk in their
sleep in the trees tonight
when the wind rattles
the branch they're on
they keep their eyes closed
to prepare for the dawn song
moth wing on the asphalt
mixed with grass shavings
and crushed stones.

YOU TELL ME
for Bob Benedict

maybe we are going some where
without the sense of moving
we think we are just standing
still but the speed is beyond
our knowledge the birds know
the rotation they follow
the currents set loose
by the spinning
something is off balance
in my head so i can't decide
which way to go
the tightness in my back
where the secret is locked
where the words hide
starting to take down the
words as they ride through
no center to speak from
no sounds in there
staring at the river
going by make the leap
into the next circle of fire
the time is right the voices
stopped talking to me
no way to tell the story
to make something up
out of air and memory.

No Accident

i don't know why it works this way
but once you find out everything
is holy there's a sadness that seeps
through your whole being like melting
snow dropping off the tree branches
settling on the ground drop by drop
buildings tumbling down in the earth
quake inside of us crashing down
hear the voices under the rubble
look in the wild horses eyes
running past steel and concrete
colliding fire hoses washing pieces
of flesh and bone off the pavement
a sadness seeps through the cracks
drifting out here trying to light
a candle for the wounded in the wind.

BURY THE DIRT

dug out the line off the back
of a postcard you wrote stuck
in the book for a marker
it said bury the dirt
dirt from the graveside
carried around for a long time
wrapped in a blue bandana.

HAMMER

HAVE MERCY

after spinning around
so many times back here
at the same spot
the guitar sounds
like the saddle
on the horse's back.

THE SONG SHOP

this old piece of vinyl ended up spinning around next to me
do you want to lose your mind jealous love made me walk through
the rain and snow with a couple of cold coney island hot dogs
in my coat pocket after the pontiac died downtown make it home
on foot or be found dead frozen solid in the doorway curled up
in a ball just like the way you started swimming in your
mother ending up a piece of frozen meat laid up along the
cyclone fence my wine soaked mind says keep moving those feet
through the slush walk past the sweet desire to sleep right
here in the ice and snow piled up in ribs at the edge of the
street there's part of a bottle of red wine by the bed up on
the third floor of the old house the wind is going to blow the
trees down the way they bend that far over my head moving
under the spin of the gust where it hits the frozen ground
the reappearing stick figure is you trudging and grinding your
teeth with the weird notion of being like this the last few
blocks are in a different movie the ice storm snags cars off
the x-way flips them over slams them into the concrete pillars
holding up the overpass pile ups on I-75 from Detroit down to
Toledo Ohio ice and wind and flying semi trailers in the gust
spinning along the interstate. my fingers don't have any
flesh on them trying to get the key in the hole the fact of a
door in front of my face that i remember as my door is the
spot in the dark the opening in the hide hanging on the sticks
in the snow where i can crawl in and make the fire turning the
key the smell of heat at the edge of the door a crack of light
in the hallway the wood steps warm my feet make the street a
distant place and time the pontiac sleeps under a blanket of
snow by now forget it she's been there before i left the radio
on when i went to get the hot dogs my ears are still frozen
and buzzing and burning at the tips i can barely hear the
hillbilly music on the radio behind the door at the top of the
stairs one more key the room is dark and warm enough to

make ice on the bottom half of the windows like a postcard
window decorated with fake ice or snow i turn up the space heater
sit down at the round oak table in the middle of the dormer
windows on three sides perched up here looking down through
the white out the loose sashes chatter and creak reach for the
bottle of red wine half fill the glass slightly stained from
before i left pull the hot dogs out of my coat pocket light a
candle and settle in to supper crooked cars and barren trees
got it together enough to be somewhere so there's a lot of dead
cars out there tonight not just mine no big deal mistake in
judgement and performance of the reliable part of this fixture
called being alive hanging in the night with this silence
filled with smoke the captive who isn't quite caught yet the
silent part of the sonata so quiet you wonder if it started or
the piano is sleeping even when the keys are pounding away in
some maniac episode digging around in the box for a roach
to fire up might as well walk to the Song Shop since i made it
here without freezing to death go listen to Bobby play the
piano and sing hillbilly songs framed in whiskey and cokes
throat notes break your heart cross hanging from a string
under his shirt.

MAP FOR RELEASE

you should have seen it coming
must have read the signs wrong
not sure what the directions
involved it wasn't written down
this time they're all still dancing
around covered with mud and sticks
i saw them in the middle of the night
no one else was around so i just stood
there like they couldn't see me sense
my presence even now it seems unreal.

Rave On
for Bobby McDonald

another cigarette trying to figure out why i inherited Bobby's
piano when i did. a cheap console piano beat up and stained
from all those years in the bar beer and whiskey poured
down into her strings soaking into the wood and iron she
has a smell of her own pieces of fake ivory broken off
the keys ruthless music through such a frail frame for a body
but then again Bobby and i connected through the poems we
were reading talking about Rimbaud and Artaud and this one
night after i got out of the draft that was more than a draft
a raging wind tearing everything down in its path blood
baptism by the war makers little did they know how deep the
resentment went somehow generated in our hearts rang out the
keys of this piano long after all that night the whole bar celebrated in
disconnected bundles of language and gestures from each
table the clanking wings of the piano chords skinny wrists like
wires sticking out of the sleeves of the fatigue jacket rising
and falling fingers set loose on the keys Bobby singing at the
edge of falsetto rave on it's a crazy feeling.
most of time i just sit here and stare out the window
thinking i'm going to figure out my next move the plan to stay
up on my feet move from here to there and back again to end
up right here figuring a plan to keep on top of the ebbs and
flows the wax and wane the freezing wind is smashing against
the door so where is there to go at least i have a door
to be behind a room to be in when it's twenty below zero
in the wind some remarkable sense of exposure to the
temporary protection the massive silence from the ground
frozen solid covered with her snow blanket conjuring the sight
of the pheasants holding to the branches like bags of feathers and
ice facing into the wind tonight.

if i could push my body through the night like that i might
be able to focus on the moment on the perfection of the
feather the fold over fold under the down the hollow stem
submerged in the skin the beating heart.
when the constants fail the door swings open and who walks
in no one you recognize at first but disappears so fast there's
no recalling what happened when the constants fail to appear
and you're swinging a pick digging through the clay until the
water starts to drip through the mud rises from the hole pulls
the pick out of your hand the surface below ground level
between the slow pack of ice and stone the voiceless voice
the great mediator who you have to wait for or not wait
but prepare without a plan the clock on the wall radiates an
illusion of progress without a sun or moon disregards the
rotation through space we do travel turns out to be standing
still a feather swinging in a limb might be your pulse the
wind pushing the feather gradually from the needles and leaves.

MANEUVERS

the tremors what we see is going on
so you are suppose to think about
the drug war the war on poverty
the war against crime and you
are the soldier sitting in front
of your TV in your helpless regalia
stunned by your stuff the war
against the poor keep flashing
the war sign so the formation
can be seen from above how
the people move around
the grid what front
are you at now break a line
on the screen and they start
to track you down.

JUNKIE SUNSET

looking over the old tapes
picking out the one
with junkie sunset on it
can you show me what's left
that's growing screaming the line
over and over again
with Moe smashing his drums
to bits and pieces
with a bandana on his head
screaming spikes in my eyesight
over and over again
Moe smashing his drums
in the homemade studio
just off Irving street
in the sunset district
making a song no one can
listen to and having the cohorts
to do it with then
heading down to the ocean
to get some wine
at this no where bar
a stone's throw from the water
going to the water
to bark at the seals
on the rock out there
in the darkness.
put the tape back
turn it off pull the shade
down on the scenery that made
that song back there crashing
on the rocks stumbling around
with a rusty guitar and broken

teeth heading to any place still
open after closing time opening
the smoking door down the stair
quick snort of methadrine
pulling a half pint
out of my pocket to wash
the singe down my throat
feel the hollow holes
where my eyes live
put up with the unraveling
footprints going nowhere
only a reflection of things
that can't be touched
the edges are sharp
defined like a map
for travel into stillness
regaining balance for an instant
then the cold moves through
my body entering my head
like a river of stones
rolling over each other
between my skin and bones
stones frozen in mud
moving then trapped when they
reach the tips of my fingers
there's a gun outside
someone evening up a grudge
for a pair of tennis shoes
and a leather coat
for christ sake
don't get caught in the cross
fire keep low when the shots
go off duck into the shadows

douse the lights stay away
from the windows
the cold moves down into
my stomach through my legs
my feet frozen in the mud
motionless trunk of flesh
next to the tree
finally falling asleep
in the park in a bundle
of sumac the wet earth
against my face the sound
of the waves washing up
on the beach in the distance
a crow caws wakes me
better get out of here
before the sun comes up
there's a coffee shop
glowing in the pre dawn
light a waitress and a few
other souls inside
as i open the door.

IF THEY ASK

when the message comes
you'll know it
there's no way
to get this order
you've been talking about
even if you think
you captured the mountain.

WHEN THE SMOKE CLEARS

all the machines are running full blast
a trail of dust and debris chewed up roots
piles of trunks the smell of diesel and thick
oil coats your lungs carcasses of birds of all
kinds laying in the muck beside the tractor
tracks gauged in the mud the black water in
still pools steaming in the heat from motors
going day and night freighters crack in half
spilling their guts out entrails washing up
on the beach cords of crude snaking the coast
collisions in space. we are being overrun
by our selves the collection box is empty
blue light before day break snow covered roof
street reflecting into the sky incessant train
hauling memories through my brain dumping
carloads of faces behind my eyes overturned
derailed battered lopsided from the load of
my own karmic cargo on this trip momentary
hook up with the static field lingering up
there in the stratosphere slow travel back
to the forest floor sun light breaking through
the thick canopy of branches and leaves even
though time has run out we're still looking
at the clock for a location in the spin i had
to head out what other choice.

AHEAD OF YOURSELF

candles burning in the hoop
of time the remarkable and
the unnoticed simultaneous
time doesn't march on just
a little different with each
dawn. throw this in the pile
get on with the real shit don't
be talking about time like you
know that you're talking about
about time to be in it you know
what i mean in time to miss
the train of thought pulling out
of the station before you got
there out of time by the time
you stepped out on the platform
looking down the track smelling
the smoke and dirt on your clothes
walking back to a hole in the ground
to rest to get up make another attempt
this time go in the opposite direction
from the way you went yesterday
this time thing has got you spinning
around from stop to stop now isn't up
to you that's why your legs ache
like they do a few steps ahead
of where you thought you were
at that time the train pulled
out a long time ago.

TWENTY FOUR HOURS

shake the dust off the continent
before the gases take over
he didn't speak no angles
waiting for the sun to come
up know it won't be soon
so waiting is not the right
word it's not an event
there are no events when the newsman
talks about the events here and there
they're not events filler in the passage
of time like a gas pump what will you
do tomorrow is sunday today is sunday
the sun is not here yet
there will be no events
you will do things with your hands
and body and mouth you speak
to others or you talk to yourself
you listen to the radio
the bus shakes by your window
the sun is somewhere else
right now it is dark and cold
at the end of winter
when the sun goes away
you start to prepare
for sleep you think
you're going to find
something new in the darkness
you walk out your door like
you know where you are going
when you get there
it's the wrong place too empty
you shouldn't have gone out

at all the place is too empty
a couple at the end of the bar
laughing in each other's face
waving their hands around
he knocks his glass over
sticks his elbow in the melted
drink the bartender gets it up
quick sets him out another one
one for her too off they go
I don't think there's a difference
between what we see and what
is there she says
well of course there is he
sips the fresh gin grins
and his eyes swim.

DOWN TIME

the page is blank
can't find the words
the doors are locked
windows busted out
the wind blows through
there is no key
doesn't make any difference
time to go somewhere else
fork in the road
went the wrong way
electric midnight turn back
the clock if you could find
the time where did you say
you were at the same old
streets burning under your
feet the page is blank
how we started out
caught dealing off the bottom
of the deck trying to break
even forgot the rules of the
game throw the cards
on the table
see where they fall
who's face is left showing
no slight of hand can
bring back another chance
to turn the other way head
back retrace your steps
down into the hole where
it all started you got
to work it out with
the hand you been dealt

we all got the death card
tucked in there the
bleak surprise always arrives
a knock on the door
a slippery road the snake
bite from the dark side
of your soul.

AT REST

the moon full tonight rose
bright but not blazing
clouds block the light
so the dome of sky glows
we took a ride down to the
river she was smooth with
reflected lights of the city
in her spikes of fire
in the water.

WHAT DAY IS IT

this is just the tip of the iceberg
what is you mean the way things
are going the whole vessel could sink
faster than we first calculated it's
so warm outside the bears don't know
where to go can't find a place to cross
over they miss their ice the ground
is too exposed where it shouldn't be
the sun won't go down today
what's that about another clogged
artery to the heart of the matter
mind numbing all the hacking going
on with a mutant strain of cell
life that lives on chicken bones
the sheep clones plead for mercy
at the gates talking in tongues
how it must feel to arrive
stake trucks at the scene
the technicians unload the surveillance
gear check radiation levels of the ground
surrounding the pulsing mounds of dirt
neutralize the sheep before another batch
shows up patches of wool blowing around
in the wind but the dogs got away
headed over the ridge
scraps of meat hanging from their
mouths we got to find every one of them
snuff them out before they bury
their teeth in some unsuspecting
shopper getting out of their car
in the parking lot dogs running
in packs bring out the infantry

rubber suits of course boots with
mirrors to bounce the lasers back
to infinity armor lugs stomping
down the isles of the K-mart
head gear and goggled eyes gas
masks in case the dog piss
is laced with anthrax.
the mechanical sky blocks out
the sun for another day
the ice storm claims control
of the whole area people dead
from carbon monoxide poisoning
trying to stay warm with heat
from glowing briquettes in the family
room read the instructions on the back
of the charcoal bag do not make fire
in the house no where for the smoke
to go fills your head in the grips
of the storm the whole system breaks
down. what are you writing in that
book random details i hear from
strangers on the street talking
like radios on the telephone radios
talking to radios the headlines blur
and pour over each other the message
impossible to read stuff like that
random details undischarged shells
sticking out of the sand when night
falls darkness doesn't arrive the sand
stays bright like the sun never left
even the ghosts had to leave in disgust
the waste of time pieces of information
i see on shreds of paper and glass
scattered around the empty house
where the doors are gone
i have to whisper this to the sky
because there are so many screaming.

TRIPLE ZERO

killing a million chickens in Hong Kong
today the bird flu out break there is no
cure kill the ducks in cages near the
chickens and any other foul just in case
kill all the cows in England going crazy
hemmed in the stock yard Dolly the sheep
clone depressed for no reason expert
experimentation confirms the gathering
of monks not a threat to further investigation
the twisted necks around the computer screens
looking for a fix when the triple zeros show
up don't be on life support or the airplane
that just took off not in an elevator
the cable broke couldn't recognize who was
in there the door closed the steel box fell
down bodies with crooked faces floated
to the ceiling the path opened wide like
the other side of the sky. all plans and
preparations lay in ruin a quivering mass
depleted of vital fluids scrapings strew
at the crash site everybody left abhorred
by the tragedy the wastefulness with so
many prospects so close at hand only a
matter of time before the bud would blossom
the door burst open the room filled
with tear gas blindness your own clothes
strangle you someone make a phone call
punch in the code first find out what
to do with the body and the hostages.

AWARDS CEREMONY
for Harvey Kubernik

yeah sitting on the couch
staring at the flashing box
what the American Music Awards
all the big sellers gather
the place smells like brand new
leather lots of it
Mariah Carey direct from Tokyo
200 thousand satellites collide
burst the bubble but no it goes on
everybody so thankful so full
of pleasure not one odd ball
in the whole lot except soy bomb
well behaved grateful to be accepting
the award thank you to my
my sick and tired attitude
about all the crumbling downess
not that coolness your highness makes
me nose dive you keep repeating yourself
it wasn't that interesting to start with
that's over they got their trophies
they keep holding them over their heads
the place smells like oily soap flakes
saturated with perfume and sweaty palms
a designer scent hanging in a cloud
over the crowd limousines waiting to go
to the afterglows hand signals twisted
fingers limbs askew half cocked heads
ways to walk to the limo doors
ways to get in lean back take in the sights
lights flash the reflection of your face
in the window is brutal and clean

sculpted lips to match reptilian boots
diamond studded teeth ah sleep. i hope
they don't turn my water off
watching the man outside in the night
carrying a couple garbage bags
over his back it's snowing and wet
in floppy tennis shoes
slipping around on the ice
somebody stole my cart mother fucker
had all my shit in it now i got to carry
the shit i got on my fucking back.
climbing in the limo a full leather suit
leather seats leather hat leather feet
leather shirt leather face but no more
beast the beasts are going away
we fucked up they're leaving
as fast as they can
but they got no where to go
even the ones that can fly
can't find a flight plan
to stay clear of all the jets
and junk up in the sky
leather socks and cocaine heart
attacks just stupid shit
the mother fucker just walked
away with my cart
all my shit
you want a cigarette.

ROAD CREW

straw cowboy hat on top of a yellow
rain pancho a slump figure behind
the controls of the CAT dozer
every knot tied by someone
sometime before now screws
and a steel skin slabs of worn out
concrete fill in the blanks
at the edge of the grid
thick and in motion from the ground up
ground down the shoe leather stepping
over the graves it's coming back to me
the train stopped the silence waiting
thickening like cornmeal boiling in on
itself it's coming back knots unravel
as the stomach empties things interlocking
things unfolding fold in on each other
shake the ashes and oil off your wings
break into flight out of the pit
of tongues there's nothing to get
no place to put it.

FOLLOW THEM HOME

the magic is everywhere
you look but you don't quite
see it you feel it and figure
you have to trust in something
the way things are going
faces arranged to suit
a garmet's grace
you would look perfect
in this reaching for the
strand of frail silk
twisting across the sky
the way sea gulls figure eight
their way toward the water.

WHO'S KEEPING SCORE

there isn't just one way to get there
you must have figured that out by now
when you say look at that do you mean
look at everything at one time pictured
in constant motion the crowd so many
waves of humans then the gun fire
the armored troop carrier is too
familiar let's go take a look at
the celebration in the locker room
you boys sure are having quite
a time in here how about pouring
some of that champagne over my head
while we talk about your win
you win you won no one
with o at the beginning
confuses everything don't want
to confuse folks with stuff like
one where they got nothing to win
but oneness no problem with that
we got them picking sides
telecast another batch
of pictures of the massacre
after the game.

SABOTAGE

home on the range
to range the root of
strange the way it is
today they all wanted
to range orange arrangements
of cold steel stuck in the
ground ready to accept a concrete
skin so that is why music
was invented to unwind
into outer space set free
from ground zero fuck up
the TV satellites.

POST MODEM

the most common part of the night
flashes of lightning rolls of thick
thunder was the static on the radio
hissing like a file pulled across
the glass table top in the fancy
waiting room where they are wandering
around like the place could explode
in their hands. flip through the pages
find the story of the quiet spot
in the middle of the abandoned city
the saplings push through the rusty
floor boards of the dead car
in a pile of weeds.

HEAL THIS UP

strong flight on the stiff winds
looking down at the iron shovel
encircled by black smoke
the river is blocked with crushed
stone and worn out tires
yellow truck pulling out
from the rest stop
with an eagle painted
on the side
the cornfields are yellow
seas the sun is eclipsed
the truck turns gray
the eagle rips at the paint
on her wings throws the truck
off the road right in front
of me.

CURTAIN

for Sherry Hendrick

after the shows are over
the dream of the magician
in the dunes teaching her way
to her students saying what
to do with the piece of silk
as big as a blanket
what to do with each move
to make the silk animate
like it has a life of its own
first flat on the ground
then vertical strung from the moon
to the dunes like a guitar string.

NAILS

PURGE THE EXCESS

high seas the threat of sharks
the thrashing machine strapped
to your brain with bailing wire
embarking on one more step
into the water to avoid revealment
stripped of your defenses.

THE AUTHORITIES

how was i suppose to interpret
what they call the facts
how could i be sure they weren't
selling me another bill of goods
saying i had a bad attitude
if i didn't take their word
for it we're telling you this is
the way it went this is how it goes
from now on you got a problem
with that keep it to yourself
come in here just relax
we're going to run a few tests
pull up your sleeve
we need to take some of your blood
just relax this won't hurt
not aware there is anything
around them but their own voice
shouting out the commands
coming back on them the echo
of the tongue in the mirror
keeps reflecting every sound
they make narrows down the chance
anything can survive unless they
can bring it up on the screen
surveille every creature for defects
then throw on the manipulation
switch shuffle a few genes
the mongrel dog escapes from the
laboratory with cat eyes.
papers pile up to no consequence
like the pile of branches
to sleep on no electric force

will change the way the stuff is
maybe you don't believe everything
is covered with oil by now maybe
you think you need to be seen by
someone to make you complete
the time might have already happened
you missed it something to say to
lose the words get everything at once.

DAWN PATROL

there are so many points of focus
i end up just sitting here staring
out the window watching the leaves
grow the rain clouds roll in the
thunder head explodes with ragged
lightning bolts the darkness falls
the sirens wail somewhere in the
distance not too near like the gun
shots again someone with a weapon
wants to hear what it sounds like
in the middle of the city
in the middle of the night
i sit here and stare out
watch the morning light arrive
out of the dark a tiny spider
making a web in front of me
on the light cord as the sun
gets ready a spider the size
of a grain of rice weaving
her web in front of me
getting ready for some one
to arrive it's a cool morning
for July.

TESTIFY

i don't remember how it went
exactly even if i did it would
only be that one way to look
at it from inside here that's
not the answer to the question
sit closer to the microphone
when you talk we want everyone
to hear this but there isn't
everyone at any one time is
there you say there is with a
weak pulse hard to feel it
hard to watch for the slightest
movement under the skin don't
doubt what we say when the final
judgement is made. single moment
of quiet outlawed in the canyons
reverberating with some sound
that resembles your voice talking
to you over the ridge from here.
the sun is nearly down for today
a very hot day with clouds floating
across the sky did they offer some
way what your prayers should look
like when they turn to water
when they turn to fire
as they leave your tongue.

SINGLE HANDED

for Steve Tudor

the perfect method to organize the pieces
the mob scene again an incidental event
set off the hair brain trigger release
the grief while they watch the replay
kicks and ragged blows to the head
to the body to the legs and feet and
broken hands and fingers beyond the place
where you even have a voice somewhere in
the flood of your own adrenaline blood
rushing everywhere it was reported
then the weather report and the story
of the sail boat under full sail
with no one on board the boat beating
against the rocky shore line single handed
Mackinac race but they couldn't find the
captain after two days they give up the
search so there he is somewhere in these
lakes maybe he's down here by the river
close to where he lived rolling with
the current down there sitting here
watching it go by trucks coming into
town rumbling motors shifting gears
between the lights making it to
the interchange not too far from
here trucks as big as bombers
from newsreels of world war two
linking up with freight or
heading home.

HIT AND RUN

woke out of the dream this morning
laying on my back in tall grass
at the edge of the trees
watching what i thought were hawks
circling over head very high
in the blue sky then just two
circling birds coming lower
with each rotation falling
near the tree tops
some animal aims at the setting sun
flight before sleep crossing over
a patch of habitation
mall makers slash and burn small
game round up for the burning
brush pile of the remains
of your home he said
not mine this time
they are eagles dark bodies
white heads white tail feathers
one staying at tree top height
the other dropping through the trees
getting bigger and much closer
hard to say at the last moment
when her wings were bigger
than my body before she touched
down on me hard to say
something i think to say
i was road kill it was
something alive with this
voice must have thought
i should stop the encounter
then woke up was still dark
outside a thin strip of light
in the east a dark weather front
hanging on the horizon.

HEART OF THE FIRE

my wings got singed that time
too close to the flame
coming down out of the sky
out of the dark clouds
cold wet wind blowing across
the land a moonless night
stealing a few more scraps
of time near the heat of the
fire crackling and spitting
sparks up into the black trees
bare in december the ache
in my shoulders to push
beyond the heart of the fire.

CAMP SITE

at the marsh spot
boiling the potato slices
in a small pot getting them
ready to fry up throw on the
fish fillets with a squeeze
of lemon in the oil
the fire down to hot coals
at the edge of the time zone
pine trees in sandy soil
have a cigarette and some coffee
after eating the smoke from the
rekindled fire pouring over me
makes the mosquitoes stay away
getting the place cleared up
wash the wooden bowls
at the trickle of water
from the water jug
out the back
of the station wagon.

RECORD RAIN

sex crimes on women
under their command
at the proving ground
sexual predators free
to strike again
streets of burning garbage
no rice no meat
riding into the town
of Goma sick and starving
civilians huddled by the
river it is a pity
he said the cost of
a multinational response
to access the damage
of the flood
where they huddle
record rain fall
the goal line on high ground
the goal posts twist under
the weight of the crowd
screaming their lungs out
for the win in their town
have a cigar and smell
this page to see if that's
how you want to smell tonight
watching the crowd go wild
in bright colors checks and
numbers team names trampling
each other in the mad rush
as the bombs start to go off
it's a pity he said
there is no way to predict
something like this happening
the flood gates only open
so far.

CALL OFF THE SEARCH

if i find the system
i'll let you know
how it works out
if i find the outlets
that lead to the big
horizon bigger than the
disaster in the lake that
makes the horizon you're
talking about the answer
never surfaced the spotlights
died away into the fog the search
was ended because nothing could be
seen in the night air as thick as
this everyone went off in their own
directions but it looked like they
were just lost but leaving because
there was nothing to be seen in a
night as blank as this one the waves
thrashed at my feet as the figures
disappeared the white teeth of the
waves flashed in a blur in the
thick fog i turned away and walked
up the rocks back to the road got
in my car and aimed for my place.

FIRE TENDER
for Lisle Earl

everything slows down
when it gets like this
the wind is constant and strong
rattling the trees together
trying to wake them up
in the frozen night
the squirrels are sleeping
in their nest curled up
together like a pile of stones
in a basket of leaves
i don't have all the details
in order yet words move slowly
into the air above the fire
a few sparks within the cosmos
is my warmth when it
gets like this.

PUNCHED IN

they were down in the mine
the wetness the cracking sound
from far above moves slowly through
the thick stone and dirt down
to where they are digging out coal
today the roof caved in on all
of them somewhere in northern Russia
they all had breakfast before dawn
the first morning after the new moon
setting out on the last phase
of this set of seasons filling
the thermos with fresh hot coffee
head out the door all the same.

IN THE WAY

the acid rain soaks my brain
metallic particles glisten
in dark light the collapse
contagious breath encountered at
the stop n shop carried home in
the plastic bag with the plastic
loaf of bread thoughts grow up
from seeds contorted misguided to
fake light in the cavity searching
for the exit becomes so obsessive
muscles ache deep below the skin
surface the unknown of your own
body threatens to take over all
movement leave you shaking
in the corner all your plans
halted before conception
it was time to go there was
no reason left to make you stay
but you just couldn't move any
thing captive of your own making
sirens wailing in the purple sunrise
block out the birds starting to sing
only at this spot where you sit
collecting your useless pieces of
logic for functioning another
plane goes down in the forest
at the edge of the airport
missed its mark the trees took
over took all the souls on board
the wings rip off the jumbo jet
enters the stand of old growth
fir trees clumped together just

talking when it happened some
got broken but only a few while
the rest stood there looked down
at the mess.

STARVE THE FEVER

the light of the fire before dawn
all descriptions year after year
the picture lacks details unexplained
deceptive to the flickering flames
the intermittent light between words
still impossible to block the flood
of information from the outside the
jittery infrastructure the heat sleep
deprivation to wear him down before
the cops move in to blow him away
it's all ugly.

DON'T GET ME WRONG

they cloned the lamb
the lion's not around
a few hiding out in what's
left of their home land
between the 4x4 tire tracks
out back in the TV set
the Jeep on the mountain top
who gives a fuck
the lamb got cloned
you're next if you make it
through the bacteria burger
on your barbecue wake up
with blood in your mouth
wasn't the second hand smoke
that did that the explosion
at the plastics plant gridlock
from here to the amazon
right above your head
the sky is blistered
cracked from frequency overload
boiling over around the cell phone
don't get me wrong
i can hear the clock ticking
i can hear the rocks rubbing
together filling steel boats
with iron ore shovel jaws biting
into the pile next to the river
don't get me wrong
when i started to talk
my face was deformed
from the words that came

out i couldn't make sense
of the sound ringing
in my skull so i just
left with my mouth
shut. you going to the
place tonight or are you
going to sleep it's only
fair don't get me wrong
how did you expect to
get anywhere with all
those cracks and tears
in the paper you can't
read the words anymore
yeah i'm going to the place
tonight you driving.

TRAP DOOR

trying to write the moon
flying song and dance disrupted
by the helicopter camouflage for
night survey the spot light makes
you blind trap door under the kitchen
table open every time the same way
the game not as high as the moon.
there are no messages left for you
the lines were cut last night
roads leading out are blocked.

SCAR

you didn't figure they'd just tear
the door off the hinges throw it out
in the street was the way you saw
your place in the line up the one
outside the entrance of your room
that night something must have
happened in there the coroner's truck
parked outside they were carrying
something out of the house zipped up
and bulky motionless weight flesh
turned to concrete stiff and remorseless
now after raising hell the story of
a broken leg drunk night crystal meth
breakfast with bloody mary down in
the china basin bugs planted in your
brain all the crops eaten or dried up
stock piled under the thundering avalanche
crawling around on all fours
through the glass.

SHAPE SHIFT

considering the driver of the red armored
truck climbing out of Delaware Gap
tucked in there behind the thick glass
riveted plate steel around him looking
out at the crystal blue sky the pine
stand stuck in the rock mustard blossoms
ringing the base of the trunks
a truck full of money locked inside there
does he think about that all the time
does he just say fuck it i'll wear
the hat his face is round and smooth
under the hat a little puffy where
his neck meets his head bent over
the wheel in the ditch one time when
he was a kid starting out in some
barn town with that first piece of
shit car he rolled like a keg of beer
over the edge but he only broke
his collar bone and cracked out
a couple front teeth he's not thinking
about that now in the red armored
truck with his hat pulled tight
the turkey vulture circles on the heat
not contingent on the car wreck
i'm road kill but i'm walking around
must have been how i returned
to this place walking up to the edge
of the highway that night looking
up the last time to find myself here
after my body got eaten up and my bones
lay there in the body of a deer

was the hoop i jumped into
jumped out of into this one
looking at one lying by the side
of the road dried blood and skin
and fur and my antlers just
starting to grow they got me
when i was running to get back
to the woods to hide out they
got me and released me when the
truck smashed into me they released
me and put me here to stare up
at the turkey vulture considering the
red armored truck.

CATS AND DOGS

dogs barking again just like the book
said they would be the moon is blazing
the cat is rolled up on the couch
doesn't pay any attention to the barking
and howling outside the perfection
of sleep rolled up in fur.

FOR REAL

i piss on the tree of knowledge
so if i come back this way i can
sniff out my trail
spending the night listening
to Kabuki and Beethoven one cut
of Noh one cut of rib from each
sonic beast airborne geography
on top of gravity bound feet
lay over here and watch the crows
pick at my flesh and listen to
their conversation of where to
build the nest laugh at something
loud enough to shock the blue jay
off the nearby branch.

FAMILY TREE

the connection was made
all the lights went out
no power to sound the sirens
the quiet prevails the faces
show up in the darkness
gather around one by one
in the clearing under the stars
collected in the black sky
carried off for some reason
with the stillness before
the storm a common place
in the night repeating
the unknown language
no signature there's nothing
to sign out here trying
to access the other place
that's it it's not a place
identified in the rules
of one dimension the clutter
in place on the mountain
to cover the power but like
the dream it rolls off
reveals the rocky skin
if i knew how
to pray to the earth
and sky and water
and stars and sun and
moon i would keep
repeating the words
until there was a calm
spot and rest and start

again but i don't know
how to pray. trying to get
at the other down the links
of the chain that rattles
in my spine starting at the
top where these words are
seeing the wind for the first
time with a face just below
here loosing ground the weight
of gravity on my grip
birds screeching over
my shoulder saying jump
let go fall into our world.

EQUAL PARTS

the thunder is rolling in late
afternoon heading into sundown
the pheasant just squawked
he must have landed
in the field
the thunder rolls again
sitting up here in the room
in the trees outside the window
across the alley the little kids
are singing some unknown song
in short segments silence
then singing again the rain
is starting to lap on the leaves
sitting here sorting through
all these pieces of paper
little pads with a few words
random addresses broken rawhide
shoelaces and a can full of sand.

TACTIC

as we ride into
the millennium sunset
i don't have a master
plan where what's happened
so far is suppose to
add up to some one
haven't i seen your face
before he kept saying
in the smoky room
eyes pressed shut to focus
one more time
on the weight and
smell of the place
where was the exit.

DARK BEFORE DAWN

are you the one
you want to be
staring in the glass
there's no reason to talk
make each entry smaller
until the blank page is complete
chronicle the ice storm
as the source of the accident
when you can't sleep
your joints are cold
and creak like the floor
in the dark before dawn
where the spasm jerks you
from the dream of the ox
laying down the yoke
in the sand by the river
heads and horns drifting across
the water shows you how
your bones connect to everything
else starting to appear beyond
so what's the punch line
to the joke of being around
and then not
watching it all from the bleachers
stuck behind a post
sight lines disrupted by the falling rocks
in the dark before dawn
i found an opening in the wall
big enough to crawl through
make it to the other side
where there's room to breathe

in the universe
and let it back out
is that the meditation you're talking about
cosmic mouth playing the saxophone
in a smoky room
way back when everything
wasn't a hamburger ad
maybe i'm wrong
just the impression
a clear note shooting out
into the starless night
nerve ends still hot
from the blast off i go again
talking about these transformations
from the distant past another mistake
to say it's gone
there's the river to rely on
in the dark before dawn
the whole scene is vibrating.
are you the one you want to be
can you settle in your own skin
look out there the room hasn't changed
you're sitting in the same chair
the air gets thinner as the crowd
collects to catch a view
of the rising star who looks confused
drugged from all the flashing lights
body guards pack tight to make sure
no one gets too close
or tries to touch the frozen hair
don't step on those shiny shoes
you might get tossed out of the place
in the middle of all this
i wander off to forget

everything they told me about
a strategy a game plan a scam
cooked up to move the rock
in front of the door
be able to get out in time
it still won't budge
i just watch the clouds collect
the wind rattles the trees
you get taken out
an unexpected change of events
put you in the circle of flames
took the wrong turn
in the metal box after all
the tests of faith
devotion to your own stupid face.

i look into the crystal ball
all i see is
a pack of wild dogs
running down the vacant street
intent on getting someplace
before the axe falls
the ground quakes snakes whisper
about the ugly man with big feet
slack jaw never saw the hole
right in front of him
fell in just when he thought
everybody knew his name
claim to fame and accident
in the nick of time
a notch on the karmic belt
he didn't anticipate.

HIDE AND SEEK

let's say you find a place to roll up in
just about disappear all that anyone
can see if they look in is a shadow
just barely see that
they leave you alone because they
don't really see you rolled up in there
you don't own anything you had a
few things once but they all fell apart
wore out got too heavy to carry around
anymore you left them behind
the thinner this blanket gets the
warmer it gets the harder it rains
the calmer it gets the rain turns
to snow it falls and falls and
it gets colder and colder the snow
piles up around the trunks
drifts in the wind in the night
no one can find you now
rolled up in there the snow piled up
all around the wind talking all night
dawn apparent even where you are
doesn't mean much to the rotation
of mass and space to surround it
 the recollection of the things you
left behind is over and done with
not even a memory useless and
remote from being in here there
were those times you threw your
arms around in rage resentment
for being breathing in and out
the air was filled with your own
blood hero worship wish books

crawling up the hill to look for
a face to put on for a couple
days mimic the photograph
so much stuff
at your fingertips pouring over
you like stale milk everything has
a smell it all starts to
smell the same the wild wings
your arms scratching
at the sky even though there was
no sky crawling up the hill
to find a way to stand the fear
pouring over you like clawed feet
you forget the possibility of
the answer reaching you in time.

OVER THE TOP

over the top
of the mountain
beauty is sleeping
you get to there
when you least
expect it
when the steps
slow down as they
approach the river
of time out over
the top of the
mountain.

Mick Vranich was born in 1946 in Wyandotte, Michigan, an industrial town ten miles downriver from Detroit. He has been writing poems and playing guitar for thirty five years. **Saw Horse** is Vranich's fourth book of poetry. He lives in Detroit with his wife, painter, Sherry Hendrick, and makes his living as a carpenter.

WORKS BY MICK VRANICH

BOOKS OF POEMS

SALAD SURREAL: DISCERNIBLE BY DISTORTION
Salad Press, Detroit 1971

RADNIK PISAR
2 x 4 Press, Detroit 1983

BOXER'S BREAK
Past Tents Press, Detroit 1987

RECORDINGS

CLOAK OF SKIN compact disc (Poetry & Music)
New Alliance Records, Los Angeles, 1993

IDOLS OF FEAR compact disc (Poetry)
New Alliance Records, Los Angeles 1993

THE BLACK BOX cassette (Poetry & Music)
Raven, Detroit 1998

REMOTE DWELLINGS cassette (Poetry & Music)
Raven, Detroit 1998